THE EMOJI ENCYCLOPEDIA

by Cordelia Evans

Simon Spotlight
New York   London   Toronto   Sydney   New Delhi

SIMON SPOTLIGHT
An imprint of Simon & Schuster Children's Publishing Division
1230 Avenue of the Americas, New York, New York 10020
This Simon Spotlight edition June 2017
The Emoji Movie © 2017 Sony Pictures Animation Inc. All Rights
Reserved. emoji® is a registered trademark of emoji company GmbH
used under license.
For information about special discounts for bulk purchases, please
contact Simon & Schuster Special Sales at 1-866-506-1949 or
business@simonandschuster.com.
Designed by Julie Robine
Manufactured in the United States of America 0517 LAK
ISBN 978-1-4814-9982-8
ISBN 978-1-4814-9983-5 (eBook)

Contents

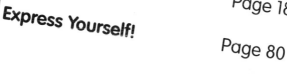

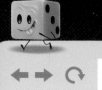

Terms and Conditions

This guide may cause laughter, astonishment, and increased texting.

Do you accept the responsibility of expressing yourself with Emojis?

If so, read on!

TEXTING...
TEXTING...1...2...3

The world of the smartphone is mysterious and magical. Isn't it mind-blowing that one little device that fits in your pocket makes your life easier? Each system, program, and app is its own little planet of perfect technology, providing necessary and crucial services to its owner.

Texting is a fast and fun way for people to get in touch. But it's not always easy. One text sent could affect your social status and reputation—there's no room for error!

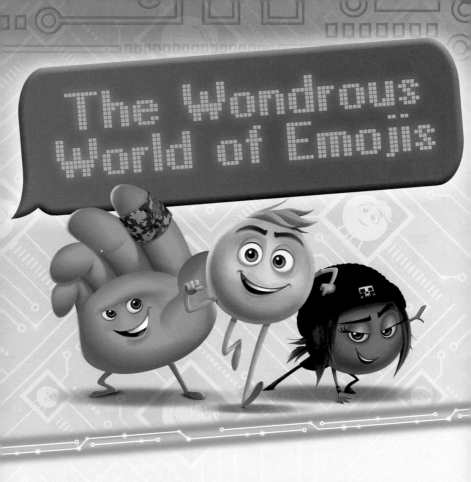

The Wondrous World of Emojis

For example, there's nothing like getting a text from a crush. At first, you're over the moon . . . but then comes the tough part: what to text back! Sometimes you can't seem to find the right words. That's when you turn to the most important invention in the history of communication . . . Emojis.

Well, maybe Emojis aren't the most important invention, but they are the most important tool when you want to show how you feel in a text.

The Lay of the Land

We can do almost anything on our smartphones—no wonder we spend so much time on them! All our apps stay neatly situated on the **wallpaper**; think of it as the land between the apps. And if the wallpaper is the landscape, then the **apps** are its buildings.

While the texting app is superpopular, other apps are waiting to help you communicate and have fun. You can post status updates on social media, share pictures, and play games (from crushing candy to dance competitions). There are also practical apps, like an antivirus app, an app for transferring files to the Cloud, and even a Trash app.

Emojis@Home

All Emojis live in **Textopolis**—
a city inside the texting app.
Emojis come together here.
Coffee Emoji and Donut Emoji
are regulars at the diner. Dog
Emojis chase Car Emojis down
the streets . . . all the time. And
if you're lucky, you might catch
Santa Claus and the Menorah
playing chess in the city park.

BE (Before Emojis)

Before our technology became advanced enough
to create today's extensive and colorful Emojis,
people used punctuation symbols to express their
emotions!

Isn't that crazy? ;)

These elderly Emoticons still live in Textopolis.

Emojis@Work

It's not just fun and games in Textopolis. When Emojis are old enough to work, they report for duty at the **Company**, where Emojis are chosen and sent up to the phone.

Like all successful organizations, the Company is run by a board. Smiler, the original Emoji, sits on the **Board**. Senior Emojis—like Devil, Lightbulb, Flamenco Dancer, and, of course, Poop—are Board Members, too. The Board Members make all the important decisions related to Emojis, including what to do when an Emoji malfunctions.

The largest and most important room in the Company headquarters is the **Theater**.

Each Emoji sits inside its own little cube, waiting to be selected. In the center of the Theater is the **Scanner**. Like a giant hand, it reaches up for the Emoji and scans its image.

Some Emojis are used way more often than others; these are the **Favorites**. Smiler is a long running Favorite. Other Favorites include Cool Sunglasses, Ice Cream Cone, Fist Bump, Peace Sign, Devil, and Angel.

There's no guarantee an Emoji will be a member of this elite group. Falling out of favor can result in a speedy demotion back to a regular cube.

Hashtag Blessed

Favorites get special treatment in the Theater. Their section is separated from the other cubes by a velvet rope, and a RAM Tech Bouncer keeps the other Emojis out. The cubes are tricked out with luxuries. It's like being on top of the world. No wonder Hi-5 wants back in so badly!

Losers' Lounge

Some Emojis almost never get picked. How often do you need to use the Line Graph Emoji? Or the Abandoned Luggage? These Emojis don't even bother to sit in cubes. Instead, they spend their days in a dimly lit storage room way down in the basement, aka the *Losers' Lounge*.

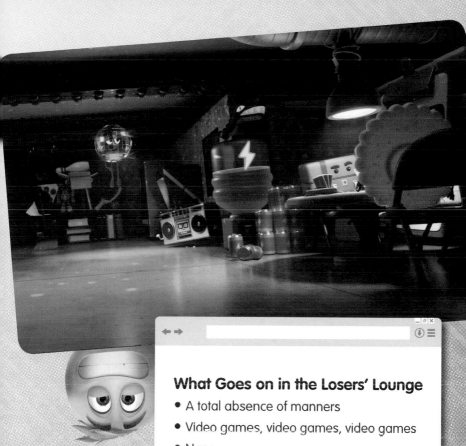

What Goes on in the Losers' Lounge
- A total absence of manners
- Video games, video games, video games
- Naps
- Endless rounds of Go Fish

Behind the Scenes

As you scroll through your Emoji bar, deciding which Emoji to send, an announcement goes out inside the Theater: **"Places, please. Emojis, to your cubes."**

The Emojis race to their cubes and try to look their best. The Scanner hovers above the cubes until an Emoji is selected.

When you finally choose an Emoji, their cube lights up and the Scanner approaches. The Emoji *must* keep still during scanning. After the scan is complete, they get sent right up to your text box.

Command Central

Inside the Company, it's the **RAM Techs** who run the show, making sure the Emoji you choose is the Emoji who gets selected. They do everything from corralling the Emojis into their cubes to defending the elite Favorites section from unwanted Emojis.

The Lead RAM Tech directs the whole process from a control room, knows exactly what you're doing on your phone (even when you're watching that cat video . . . again), and keeps the whole Theater updated on where your thumb is heading. Emojis need to be ready.

You Have One Job to Do

According to Smiler, Emojis have one job to do: wait in their cubes and be themselves! That is why Smiler is always smiling and always happy. Always.

But it's not quite as simple for some Emojis. There is that nerve-racking moment when an Emoji has been selected and is waiting to be scanned. What if the Emoji moves just a little bit?

Or—horror of horrors—*expresses a different emotion?*

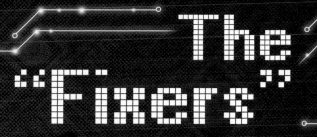

The "Fixers"

The **AV Bots** are Smiler's high-tech henchmen. They're motto is: Delete the Malfunction. And they're really good at tracking Emojis, even when they leave Textopolis and venture into the Wallpaper and the other apps.

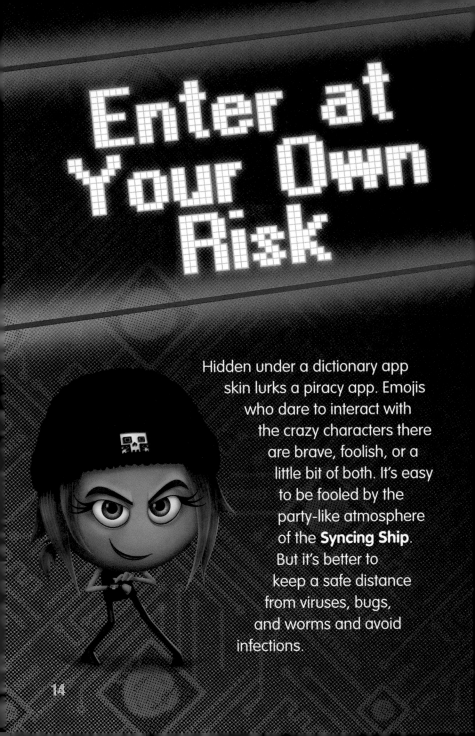

Enter at Your Own Risk

Hidden under a dictionary app skin lurks a piracy app. Emojis who dare to interact with the crazy characters there are brave, foolish, or a little bit of both. It's easy to be fooled by the party-like atmosphere of the **Syncing Ship**. But it's better to keep a safe distance from viruses, bugs, and worms and avoid infections.

Below are a few other Pirate's Code patrons to avoid.

Internet Trolls

Goal: get your attention.
Method: feeding off your emotions.
How to Deal: ignore them!

Spam

Goal: steal your identity.
Method: convince you she's your BFF.
How to Deal: don't tell her anything!

Trojan Horse

Goal: get into your system.
Method. the art of disguise.
How to Deal: trust the Trojan Soldier instead.

The Great Beyond

At the bottom of the phone is a place where no Emoji wants to end up: the **Trash**. This dirty garbage pit is filled with everything that you no longer want on your phone, from old photos, to apps you don't want to use anymore, to malware that you've deleted.

Things in the Trash are still on the phone and could come back to haunt you . . . like embarrassing emails. But once the Trash is emptied, there's no coming back!

The **Firewall** is the door to the world outside the phone. It's password protected but not totally impenetrable—as any hacker worth her skullcap knows.

Hashtag Obvious

These are some totally obvious passwords. *Avoid, avoid, avoid.*

Pet's name
Grandma's name
Favorite video game
School mascot
Name of crush

Once you're off the phone, you're in the **Cloud**; the Cloud houses all the source codes for the phone. Compared to Textopolis, it's an overwhelming sprawling metropolis.

MEET THE

EMOJIS

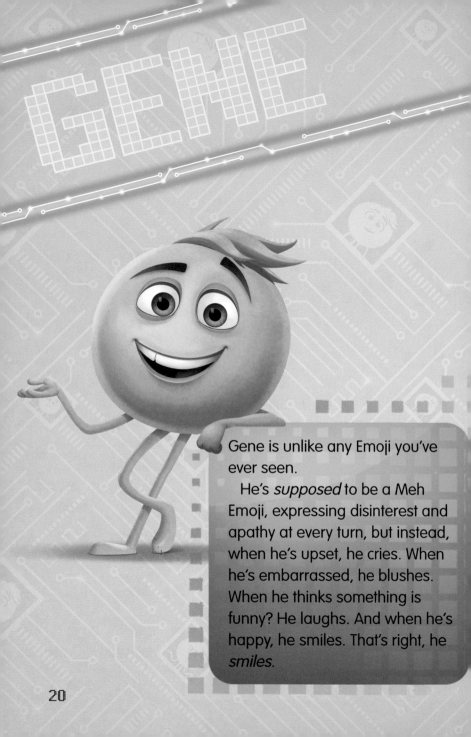

Gene is unlike any Emoji you've ever seen.

He's *supposed* to be a Meh Emoji, expressing disinterest and apathy at every turn, but instead, when he's upset, he cries. When he's embarrassed, he blushes. When he thinks something is funny? He laughs. And when he's happy, he smiles. That's right, he *smiles*.

Usefulness: 5 stars
Pair with Heart and you get: Overwhelmed with love!

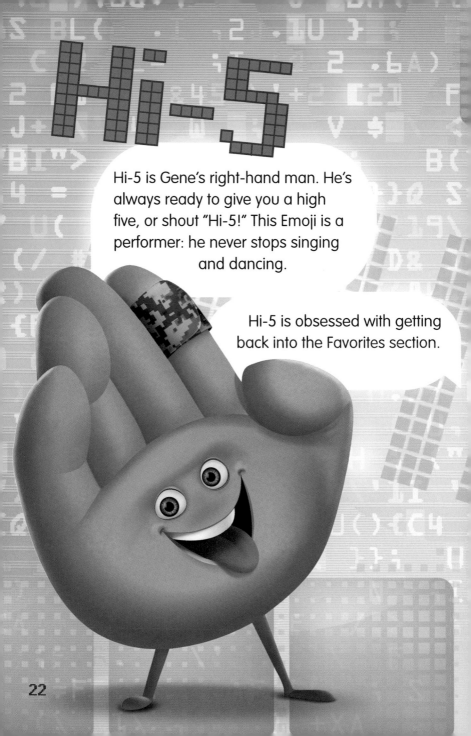

Hi-5

Hi-5 is Gene's right-hand man. He's always ready to give you a high five, or shout "Hi-5!" This Emoji is a performer: he never stops singing and dancing.

Hi-5 is obsessed with getting back into the Favorites section.

22

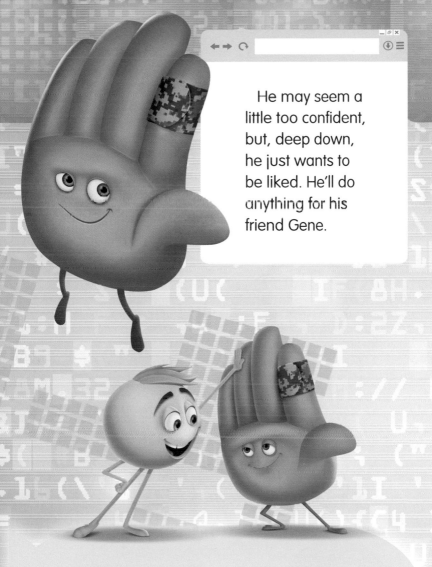

He may seem a little too confident, but, deep down, he just wants to be liked. He'll do anything for his friend Gene.

Usefulness: 5 stars
Pair with Laughing Crier and you get:
Awesome joke, dude!

Jailbreak

From her purple hair to her wrist computer, Jailbreak is one of the coolest Emojis. She's smart, funny, and knows how to get what she wants. She's a great Emoji to have on your side.

Usefulness: 5 stars
Pair with Guitar and you get: An indie rock princess!

24

Mel and Mary Meh

It's no wonder that Gene is nervous on his first day of work at the Company—he's got big expressions to fill! His parents, Mel and Mary, are the masters of Meh.

Mel and Mary are nervous on Gene's first day too (not that you could tell from their expressions). They love their son, but they're not sure Gene is going to be able to remain Meh.

Usefulness: 4 stars
Pair with Gene and you get: Meh, family.

Smiler

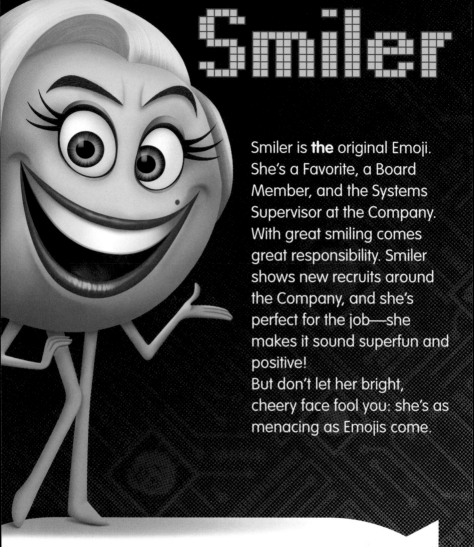

Smiler is **the** original Emoji. She's a Favorite, a Board Member, and the Systems Supervisor at the Company. With great smiling comes great responsibility. Smiler shows new recruits around the Company, and she's perfect for the job—she makes it sound superfun and positive!

But don't let her bright, cheery face fool you: she's as menacing as Emojis come.

Usefulness: 5 stars
Pair with Poop and you get: Congratulations on your number two!

ALL THE FEELS

These Emojis love to toy with your emotions. That's all they do. Together they're a powerful tool. A few standouts—like Hysterical Laughter, or Crier—are so popular they've broken away from the pack.

Usefulness: 3 stars
Combine them and you get: The many moods of me.

Angel

Nerd

Wink

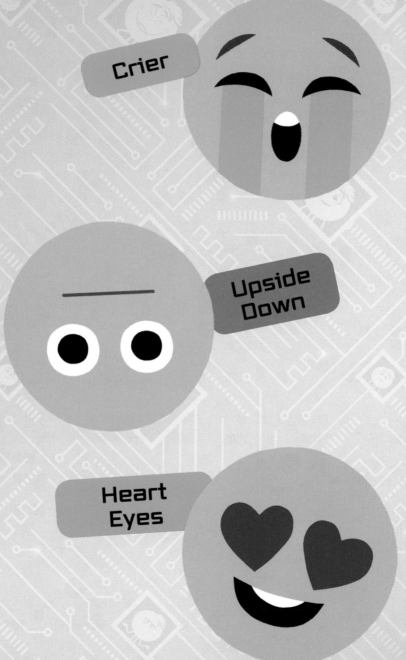

Crier

Upside Down

Heart Eyes

Angry

Sleeping

Winky Tongue
Out

Dead

Neutra-Straight Face

Scream

Eye Roll

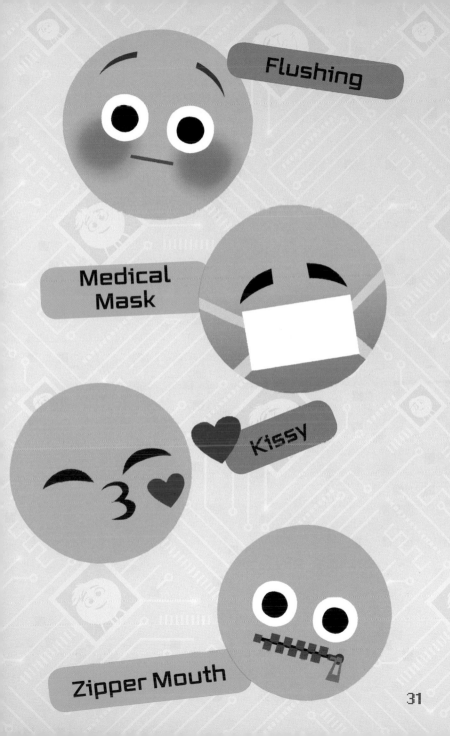

Flushing

Medical
Mask

Kissy

Zipper Mouth

31

CAT-EGORICALLY CUTE

These cool cats are some of the most **meow-erful** Emojis in Textopolis. When you can't quite figure out what to say, the cats have got your back.

Usefulness: 5 stars
Combine them and you get: Purr-fect!

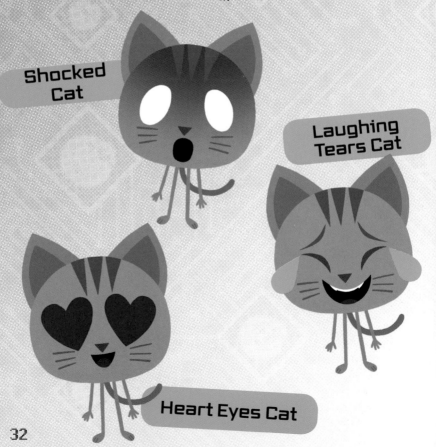

Shocked Cat

Laughing Tears Cat

Heart Eyes Cat

Bicep

Bicep is always pumped and ready to do the heavy lifting at the Company.

Usefulness: 2 stars
Pair with Elephant and you get: Don't know my own strength!

Briefcase

The most professional and organized of all the accessory Emojis, Briefcase is ready to carry text messaging to the next level.

Usefulness: 2 stars
Pair with Clock and you get: Ready for work!

Clapping Hands

Let's have a round of applause! Clapping Hands recognizes the achievements of all the Emojis in Textopolis, even though his hands hurt sometimes.

Usefulness: 4 stars
Pair with Christmas Tree and you get: Happy holidays!

Couple in love

These two just can't hide their love for each other. They're the most adorable couple in all of Textopolis. It's PDA all day.

Usefulness: 3 stars
Pair with Calendar and you get: Save the date!

Crier

It's impossible to cheer up Crier. He always has to cry, even if he's just won the lottery! He is big on staying hydrated.

Usefulness: 4 stars
Pair with Snowboarder and you get: I should stick to the bunny hill.

Devil and Devil Jr.

Devil is a perennial favorite. You would think that would mean that he'd be relaxed and keep to himself, but nope! In true devil fashion, he spends his days doing mischievous things, like poking Puppy with his pitchfork.

Speaking of the Devil . . . he's carrying on his legacy with his son, Devil Jr., a recent recruit. Hopefully, he won't follow his dad's hoof steps!

Usefulness: 4 stars
Pair with Caught Red-Handed and you get: Stirring up trouble.

Ears

This Emoji is all ears! He hears about everything that goes on in Textopolis, 'cause he's a very good listener.

Usefulness: 2 stars
Pair with Monkey and you get: I've got a secret!

Eyeballs

Eyeballs is a real looker. He sees everything that goes on in Textopolis with his own eyes.

Usefulness: 2 stars
Pair with Movie Clapper and you get: It's showtime!

Fist Bump

A literal knucklehead, Fist Bump is Hi-5's rival in both careers and love. Not only did he knock Hi-5 out of the Favorites section, but he also started dating Peace as soon as she dumped Hi-5.

Usefulness: 4 stars
Pair with Line Graph and you get:
You got this math test!

Flamenco Dancer

A very popular Emoji—so popular she's a Board Member—Flamenco Dancer has all the right moves, even if Smiler pushes her out of the room when she uses them!

Usefulness: 5 stars
Pair with Fire and you get: Hot dance moves!

Hysterical Laughter

Have you ever laughed so hard you cried? That's what Hysterical Laughter spends his time doing! But he's not wrong—it **is** hilariously funny when the Elephant Emoji stands next to the Wind Emoji!

Usefulness: 5 stars
Pair with Camera and you get:
Most hilarious picture ever!

Lips

Lips is a popular body part Emoji, especially because she always has words, whistles, or laughs flowing through her.

Usefulness: 2 stars
Pair with Wink and you get:
Love ya!

Lipstick

A close, personal friend of Lips, Lipstick really knows how to make her mark.

Usefulness: 1 star
Pair with Kiss and you get: Pucker up!

Nose

Nose is nothing to sniff at, but she does sometimes stick herself where she doesn't belong.

Usefulness: 2 stars
Pair with Flower and you get:
Stop and smell the roses!

Old Man

Old Man is really enjoying his retirement. He spends his days in the park, painting with Palette.

Usefulness: 3 stars
Pair with Old Lady and you get: Grandparents!

Old Lady (Felicia)

Old Lady spends her days playing cards in the Losers' Lounge with Eggplant, Fish Cake with Swirl, and others. She can be a real card shark.

Usefulness: 5 stars
Pair with Hi-5 and you get: Bye, Felicia!

Peace

Peace is so cool and popular, all the hand sign Emojis want to date this groovy girl. When Hi-5 was a Favorite, Peace went out with him. But as soon as he stopped being a Favorite, she peaced out on him.

Usefulness: 5 stars
Pair with Alien and you get:
We come in peace.

Sunglasses

If you haven't heard of Sunglasses, you must be living under a rock. After all, he's the coolest expression Emoji out there! So cool that he wears his sunglasses inside his cube in the Theater, which just happens to be a prime cube in the Favorites section, of course!

Usefulness: 5 stars
Pair with Volleyball and you get: A day at the beach!

Poop and Poop Jr.

The Poops family is wildly popular. Papa Poop is a Board Member and a Favorite—living life way above the toilet bowl in the elite group of cubes. The family even has a family cheer: "We're number two! We're number two!"

Usefulness: 5 stars
Pair with Slobbering Puppy and you get: Doggy doodie duty!

Princess Row

The Princesses don't have to do much to be Emoji royalty. They sit in their cubes looking pretty, making sure their hair is combed and their crowns are on straight, and . . . that's about it.

Usefulness: 3 stars

Pair with Ambulance and you get:
A royal pain!

Hashtag Princess Problems

Because the Princesses are so popular, there's a lot of gossip about them. Everyone speculates whether or not Birds actually do fly down when a Princess whistles. And all the other Emojis can't help asking why one of the Princesses' cubes is empty.

Thumbs-Up
and
Thumbs-Down

Thumbs-Up is the eternal optimist who is always finding the good in things and looking on the bright side, unlike her fraternal brother, Thumbs-Down, who is quick to point out when you've done something wrong and is always finding the worst thing about every situation.

Usefulness: 5 stars
Combine together with Gavel and you get:
A hung jury.

Two Dancing Girls

Two Dancing Girls are double trouble! They are also twice the fun and really know how to liven up a party!

Usefulness: 5 stars
Pair with Heart and you get: BFFs!

EMOJIS IN THE WILD

Alien

Aliens might not actually exist on Earth, but they do exist in Textopolis! This out-of-this-word Emoji gels along well with some old video game Emojis. After all, aliens once invaded their games!

Usefulness: 3 stars
Pair with White Flag and you get: We surrender to the invasion!

45

Bird

Did you know that when a Princess whistles, Birds fly down from the sky and land on her shoulder? Bird sure is loyal to his royalty!

Usefulness: 3 stars
Pair with Ear and you get:
A little birdie told me . . .

Cactus

Resilient Cactus thrives almost anywhere, which is good because he's stuck in the Losers' Lounge.

Usefulness: 2 stars
Pair with Ambulance and you get: Ouch!

Christmas Tree

Oh, Christmas Tree, oh, Christmas Tree! Twinkly, festive Christmas Tree positively glows on the job.

Usefulness: 4 stars
Pair with Cookie and you get: Christmas cookies!

Elephant

Stomp! Slomp! That's not an earthquake; it's just Elephant. Don't let his size fool you—he's really a gentle giant.

Usefulness: 3 stars
Pair with Wind and you get: A toot!

Fir Tree

Fir Tree spends most of his time in the Losers' Lounge. He's okay with that. It's hard for him to be near Christmas Tree and not want to take a few ornaments.

Usefulness: 2 stars
Pair with Slobbering Puppy and you get: You're barking up the wrong tree!

Flame

Flame is on fire! Literally. Whenever you see this guy, Fire Truck can't be too far behind.

Usefulness: 4 stars
Pair with Balloon and you get:
A hot-air balloon ride.

Frog

When it's time to get to work,
Frog knows how to hop to it!
He'll never admit it, but Frog
secretly pines for one of the
Princesses.

Usefulness: 1 star
Pair with Kissy Face and you get:
    You have to kiss a lot of trogs . . .

Ghost

All appearances aside, Ghost
is very friendly. He's particularly
popular in the fall but can still
conjure up some surprises year-round.

Usefulness: 2 stars
Pair with Weary and you get:
A bad dream kept me up last night.

49

Globe

Globe spins 'round and 'round but never gets tired or dizzy.

Usefulness: 2 stars
Pair with Rocket and you get:
Out of this world!

Jack-o'-lantern

Jack-o'-lantern is part of a weekly chess game with some other holiday-themed Emojis. And he'd like to clarify that it's not his fault there's no plain pumpkin Emoji.

Usefulness: 2 stars
Pair with Coffee and you get:
A pumpkin spice latte.

Monkeys

Hear No Evil, See No Evil,
Speak No Evil—that's the Monkeys' motto!
Use these guys separately or together to achieve
different effects.

Usefulness: 5 stars
Pair with Briefcase and you get:
  Monkey business!

Moon and Sun

Opposites attract when it comes to the Moon and Sun families. These two families are totally in sync but rarely seen together.

Usefulness: 1 star

Combine them and you get:

A total eclipse.

Skull

Skull may look scary, but he's just misunderstood. He can't help it if his eyes glow red and he only has half a mouth!

Usefulness: 5 stars
Pair with Jack-o'-lantern and you get: Two scary dudes.

Slobbering Puppy

Slobbering Puppy spends a lot of time chasing his tail and is afraid of Shocked Cat.

Usefulness: 4 stars
Pair with Clapping Hands and you get: Good boy!

Wind

Wind is often seen following Elephant—together, they make a toot! When you're tired, it's really helpful to have a second wind around.

Usefulness: 3 stars
Pair with Flame and you get: Blow out the candles!

Voodoo Mask

What's behind Voodoo Mask's mask? It's better not to know.

Usefulness: 1 star
Pair with One Hundred and you get: Nice Halloween costume!

Cake

Vanilla, chocolate, red velvet. Icing, whipped cream, fruit on top. Cake comes in a variety of flavors, each one yummier than the last.

Usefulness: 3 stars
**Pair with Peace and
 you get:** Piece of cake!

Cheese

Cheese may be full of holes, but she's still a big deal in Textopolis—after all, she's the big cheese!

Usefulness: 4 stars
**Pair with Smiler and you
 get:** You're so cheesy.

55

Coffee

Just as it is in the world off the phone, Coffee is very in demand in Textopolis. He's always there for his buddy, Donut. But watch out—if he's used too often, he gets a little edgy.

Usefulness: 5 stars
Pair with Sleeping and you get:
I need to wake up!

Cookie

Sweet yet tough, Cookie is the Emoji no one can crumble. An excellent student, this Emoji is one sharp cookie.

Usefulness: 3 stars
Pair with Thumbs-Up and you get:
These are delicious!

Donut

Donut and Coffee go together like . . . well, donuts and coffee. They keep each other company during the late shift.

Usefulness: 2 stars
Pair with Coffee and you get: The breakfast of champions.

Eggplant

Eggplant is stuck in the Losers' Lounge, where he's found his calling playing old-school video games.

Usefulness: 2 stars
Pair with Cheese and you get:
Eggplant Parmesan.

Fortune Cookie

A close friend of Crystal Ball, Fortune Cookie has the inside scoop on the future. Now if only we could get that inside scoop out of her!

Usefulness: 4 stars
Pair with Thumbs-Up and you get: Good luck!

A FRIEND

Fried Shrimp

Ready for any occasion, Fried Shrimp is very popular on the party circuit.

Usefulness: 2 stars
Pair with Cookie and you get: Sweet and savory.

Ice Cream Cone

I scream, you scream . . . even Scream is screaming for Ice Cream Cone! This swirly swoop of soft serve is so popular she's achieved Favorite status.

Usefulness: 4 stars
Pair with Calendar and you get: Sundaes on Sunday.

Pizza

Pizza is a real homeslice. But consider yourself warned: his jokes can be extremely cheesy.

Usefulness: 4 stars
Pair with Balloon and you get: Pizza party!

Sushi Combo

With all of life's ups and downs, the sushi Emojis have learned to just roll with it—except Fish Cake with Swirl. He's a little more sensitive and tends to spend his days in the Losers' Lounge.

Usefulness: 2 stars
Combine them and you get:
A Bento box!

Bow and Arrow

This projectile Emoji is always right on target. Use Bow and Arrow by pulling back, taking aim, and releasing your shot . . . via text, of course.

Usefulness: 2 stars
Pair with Heart and you get: Cupid in training.

Dice

Go ahead, roll Dice! If you're really lucky, maybe he'll give you snake eyes.

Usefulness: 4 stars
Pair with Angry and you get: No dice!

Disco Ball

This once-popular party accessory now spends most of her time hanging around the Losers' Lounge. Still sparkly, Disco Ball is always up for a spin on the dance floor.

Usefulness: 2 stars
Pair with Flamenco Dancer and you get:
Let's boogie on the dance floor!

Game Controller

Don't be fooled by Game Controller's happy demeanor. It's just fun and games for her, and she rarely wants to give up control!

Usefulness: 3 stars
Pair with Snowboarder and you get:
Let's hit the virtual slopes!

Make Music

Guitar, Trumpet, and Drum are the most popular instruments in Textopolis. They can riff together at a moment's notice and love to play parties, even if Trumpet is prone to tooting his own horn.

Usefulness: 3 stars

Combine them and you get: A jazz trio.

Palette

Palette loves helping other Emojis express themselves through their art! Bright and cheery, she lends her colors to paintings everywhere.

Usefulness: 2 stars
Pair with Calendar and you get: A colorful day.

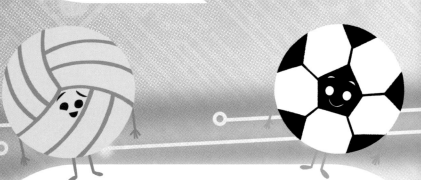

Sportsapalooza

They shoot, spike, and score. It doesn't matter if it's a pickup game or the championship—these balls always wear their game faces.

Usefulness: 3 stars
Combine them and you get: The balls are in your court.

Abandoned Luggage

It's clear to see why this Emoji has abandonment issues. Abandoned Luggage spends his days in the Losers' Lounge and sometimes acts out by taking what's not his or resorting to childish behavior.

Usefulness: 1 star
Pair with Angry and you get:
My souvenirs were in there!

Balloon

Balloon is loyal and won't ever fly away from Textopolis! Some Emojis have been known to use Balloon to get to places more quickly when they are running late.

Usefulness: 4 stars
Pair with Hammer and you get:
Pop!

Bathtub

Bathtub may not have massage jets (or even a shower curtain), but he's got his strengths. After all, he's one of the cleanest Emojis you'll ever meet!

Usefulness: 2 stars
Pair with Nose and you get: Someone needs a bath!

Bomb

Sparks fly around this little guy, but be careful—you don't want to set him off! Bomb has quite an explosive personality.

Usefulness: 3 stars
Pair with Sunglasses and you get: Supercool.

Broom

Handy, helpful, but not flashy, Broom flies under the radar—unless it's Halloween. Then Broom takes flight.

Usefulness: 1 star
Pair with Basketball and you get: A clean sweep!

Calendar

Whether she's keeping appointments or keeping track of what day it is, Calendar helps any phone user stay on schedule. Ask her to pencil you in!

Usefulness: 4 stars
Pair with Heart and you get: Valentine's Day.

Camcorder

Whenever something big happening in Textopolis, Camcorder manages to capture it all, whether it's the news or a film being shot on location.

Usefulness: 2 stars
Pair with Couple in Love and you get: A cinematic love story!

Clock

Clock is never late to anything. She's got all the time in the world . . . literally. She is made up of time.

Usefulness: 4 stars
Pair with Cake and you get: Happy birthday!

Crystal Ball

Crystal Ball has magical powers: She can see into the future! Or at least, she claims to be able to . . . Some of her predictions tend to be a little obvious.

Usefulness: 3 stars
Pair with Basketball and you get: You're going to win tonight!

Gavel

Gavel brings all the Board Meetings at the Company to order. He can be clumsy, though, what with all that banging himself around everywhere.

Usefulness: 3 stars
Pair with Caught Red-Handed and you get: A guilty verdict.

Hammer

Hammer is very handy.
Essential in any Emoji toolbox,
he can pound away at anything
from two-by-fours to coconuts!

Usefulness: 3 stars
Pair with Thumbs-Up and you get:
Nailed it!

Lightbulb

Lightbulb illuminates life in
Textopolis as a Board Member.
A fan of mysteries, Lightbulb
likes foreshadowing and expresses
himself by getting brighter or dimmer.

Usefulness: 4 stars
Pair with Thinking Face and you get: I have an idea!

A Full Deck

These Emojis are such cards . . . literally! Heart is the most popular because he speaks the universal language of love, but the other suits mostly show their poker faces, especially when Joker is acting wild.

Usefulness: 3 stars
Combine them and you get: I'm holding all the cards.

Menorah

You'll often find Menorah playing an intense game of chess with Santa Claus, Jack-o'-lantern, or Rabbit. But when winter rolls around, Menorah gets to work with assistance from Flame.

Usefulness: 3 stars
Pair with Calendar and you get:
Eight crazy nights.

Money with Wings

Money may not grow on trees, but Money with Wings can detinitely fly away! Keep your eye on this stack of cold hard cash.

Usefulness: 4 stars
Pair with Crier and you get:
I spent my allowance already.

Office Supplies

Sometimes, you need practical Emojis, like the Folders. They're a great place for Briefcase to keep all his important files—except for Line Graph, who's resigned to killing time in the Losers' Lounge.

Usefulness: 2 stars
Combine and you get: A desk set.

One Hundred

Not that anyone is keeping score in Textopolis, but if they were, the One Hundred Emoji would be winning. One Hundred celebrates everyone's accomplishments, not just her own!

Usefulness: 5 stars

Pair with Angel and you get: A perfect score.

Peace Sign

Though they share a first name, Peace Sign is very different from Peace. He's not fickle when it comes to love; he loves everyone! It helps him keep his peace of mind.

Usefulness: 3 stars

Pair with Nerd and you get: Peace of mind.

Red Wagon

Red Wagon is stuck down in the Losers' Lounge, where he patiently waits for retro toys to become cool again.

Usefulness: 2 stars
Pair with Jack-o'-lantern and you get: A Halloween haul.

Rocket

Rocket lives in a house shaped like—
you guessed it—a rocket. As Rocket waits to be scanned, he pretends it's time for liftoff. "Ten . . . nine . . . eight . . ."

Usefulness: 4 stars
Pair with Alien and you get: Life on Mars.

Stop Sign

This Emoji will stop at nothing . . . to get the other Emojis to obey traffic laws in Textopolis! Stop Sign's red color may make him seem angry, but he is really just very concerned about safety.

Usefulness: 4 stars
Pair with Annoyed and you get: Stop bothering me!

EXPRESS YOURSELF!

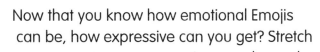

Now that you know how emotional Emojis can be, how expressive can you get? Stretch your own creative muscles and learn about how you'd fare in Textopolis by completing these fun quizzes and activities!

QUIZ:
COULD YOU OUTRUN THE AV SQUAD?

Gene and Hi-5 manage to make it all the way off the phone before being captured by the AV Squad. How far would you get? Take this quiz to find out!

1. Smiler has declared that you're a malfunction and must be deleted. What do you do?
   a. Plead with the Poop Emoji to fight for you.
   b. Hide behind a tree Emoji to sneak past the AV Bots and get out of Textopolis.
   c. See if you can camouflage yourself among the Emojis in the Losers' Lounge.

2. The AV Squad finds you in the Syncing Ship. Which malware do you send to fight them?
   a. Spam—because she seems really clever and quick thinking.
   b. The Pirates—because they're very brave.
   c. The Internet Trolls—because they could really break the Bots down.

3. You're in the Wallpaper and the AV Bots are right on your tail. What's the best app to enter?
   a. The video app—they get distracted by the cute cat videos!
   b. The dance app—they probably can't dance as well as you can.
   c. The pictures app—they'll never find you among all those selfies.

4. What is the most important thing to remember about the AV Bots?
   a. They have lasers!
   b. They can always find you.
   c. They only know one sentence.

5. How do you best avoid getting hit by the AV Bots' lasers?
   a. Hide.
   b. Run as fast as you can.
   c. Duck—they'll hit one another instead!

SCORECARD

Give yourself points according to the following chart:

	a	b	c
1	2	3	1
2	2	1	3
3	3	1	2
4	2	3	1
5	1	2	3

5–7 Points: You've Been Deleted!
You just couldn't get away from the AV Bots fast enough. Maybe someone will come dig you out of the Trash!

8–11 Points: You Almost Made It!
You were so close to getting off the phone, but they caught you at the Firewall.

12–15 Points: Welcome to the Cloud!
You made it all the way off the phone without being captured by the AV Squad. Congratulations!

DO YOU WANT TO BE A CODER LIKE JAILBREAK?

Hey, guys! It's me, Jailbreak. You know how I learned to code, and then I was able to do things like reprogram certain Emojis? Well, you can learn to code too!

Writing code is basically telling a computer what to do or programming a computer to get it to do what you want. You see, computers—and remember, a smartphone is a minicomputer!—are made up of on/off switches called transistors. When you're telling a computer what to do, you're really telling the computer which switches to turn on and which switches to turn off. This on/off language is called binary code, and it's the only language the computer understands.

Do you want to try converting something into binary code? How about LOL?

First, we have to find each letter's corresponding number via an ASCII conversion chart. This chart assigns each letter a number that can be converted into a binary number. So we need the ASCII numbers for *L* and *O*, which are 76 and 79.

Now, let's work on converting those numbers into binary numbers. A binary number is eight characters in length, and each character is either a 0 or a 1. You can determine whether each character is a 0 or a 1 using the chart on the next page. For *L*, you need to make the number 76 by adding up the numbers given to you in the left column on the chart. If you're going to use the number to get to 76, mark a 1 in the box. If you're not, mark a 0.

128	
64	
32	
16	
8	
4	
2	
1	

128	
64	
32	
16	
8	
4	
2	
1	

Write your eight character binary number here:

__ __ __ __ __ __ __ __

Now, do the same thing for the number 79 to find out what the binary number for O is.

Write your eight character binary number here:

__ __ __ __ __ __ __ __

Now, fill in the blanks below to find out what LOL is in binary code!

__ __ __ __ __ __ __ __   __ __ __ __

__ __ __ __   __ __ __ __ __ __ __ __

Congratulations! You just took the first step in learning to code. If you want to learn more, ask a parent, teacher, or librarian.
Answer: 01001100 01001111 01001100

QUIZ: WHO WOULD BE YOUR BEST EMOJI BUD?

Which Emoji do you think you'd hit it off with? Take this quiz to find out!

1. How would you describe your best friend?
    a. Funny and lovable.
    b. Energetic and goofy.
    c. Smart and determined.
    d. A big softy.

2. Pick the activity that best describes how you'd like to spend your Saturday.
    a. Hanging out with family and friends.
    b. Learning some new dance moves.
    c. Programming a new computer game.
    d. Working on an extra-credit assignment to make my teacher happy.

3. What's your biggest dream?
    a. To be able to be myself no matter what.
    b. To be everyone's favorite person.
    c. To have my own apartment.
    d. To win over Smiler.

4. Do you care about being popular?
   a. Meh, I care more about true friendship.
   b. Absolutely, it's my biggest priority.
   c. No. Go away. I'm very busy.
   d. I'm very popular, but I try not to let it get to my head.

5. How loyal would you say you are?
   a. Very—I put my friends' happiness ahead of mine.
   b. I'm loyal when it really matters.
   c. I do my own thing, but I'm there for my friends when they need me.
   d. I'm just flush with loyalty!

SCORECARD

Mostly As: Gene
You're loyal and sincere. You and Gene would be true-blue friends!

Mostly Bs: Hi-5
You love to have fun—you and Hi-5 would have a blast together.

Mostly Cs: Jailbreak
You're independent and cool, but you could still use a friend like Jailbreak.

Mostly Ds: Poop
You'd get along great with Mr. Number Two!

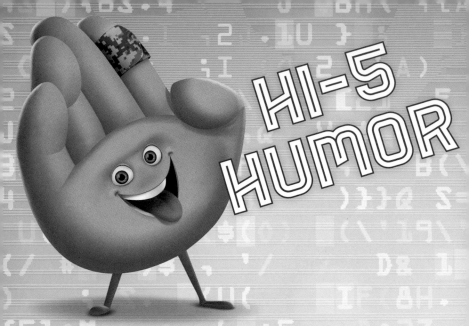

HI-5 HUMOR

Want to make your friends laugh just like Hi-5? Check out this collection of his best jokes!

Q: Why do all the Emojis keep sneezing?

A: There's a computer virus going around!

Q: What happened to the Emoji who kept daydreaming?

A: She lost her head in the Cloud.

Q: What did one Emoji say to the other?

A: "I'm so hungry, I could eat a megabyte!"

Q: Why did the Emoji forget her mom's birthday?

A: She ran out of memory.

Q: Why didn't the girl delete her selfie?

A: She didn't want to send herself to the Trash!

Q: What's the fastest way to spread news?

A: Word of mouse.

Q: Why did the boy put airbags on his computer?

A: In case it crashed!

Q: How are things measured on a phone?

A: By length and bandwidth.

Q: What do you call it when an Emoji takes off her shoes and then puts them on again?

A: A reboot.

QUIZ: WHICH EMOJI ARE YOU?

Out of the hundreds of Emojis, which one are you most like?
Take this quiz to find out!

1. What's your favorite type of movie?
   a. Comedy, of course.
   b. Film noir.
   c. Anything with animals—I just LOVE animals!
   d. Any movie where the good guy wins in the end.

2. What would your teacher say about you?
   a. I'm the class clown.
   b. I'm too cool for school.
   c. I'm very enthusiastic.
   d. I'm the perfect student.

3. You have a fight with your sister, but you realize you were wrong. What do you do?
   a. Admit it right away; it's pretty funny, now that I think about it!
   b. Keep quiet. I don't want to ruin my reputation.
   c. Tell her she was right and I'm sorry. I LOVE my sister, and I'd never want to hurt her!
   d. That would never happen. I'm never wrong.

4. What's your favorite holiday?
   a. April Fool's Day.
   b. The 4th of July.
   c. Valentine's Day.
   d. Christmas Day.

5. If your friend was really upset about not getting a solo in the orchestra's concert, what would you do to cheer him up?
   a. Tell him jokes until he cracked a smile.
   b. Tell him he's too cool for orchestra anyway.
   c. Give him a big hug!
   d. Remind him how much he loves orchestra and how he'll have another shot.

SCORECARD

Mostly As: Hysterical Laughter Emoji
You can find the funny in any situation, just like this Emoji, who never stops laughing.

Mostly Bs: Sunglasses Emoji
You wear your sunglasses all the time, just like the Sunglasses Emoji—you're too cool not to!

Mostly Cs: Cat Heart Eyes Emoji
You just LOVE your friends and your pet and school, and . . . pretty much everything!

Mostly Ds: Angel Emoji
You're pretty much perfect in every way, just like the Angel Emoji. Well, she actually IS perfect in every way.

SUCCESS!

Information upload complete

You've learned everything there is to know about Emojis and what life is like for them in Textopolis!

From the Theater inside the Company, to the Wallpaper and Apps, through the Firewall and all the way up to the Cloud, you've seen how it all happens: how all the intricate inner systems in your phone work together to help you send one simple text that expresses so much.

After all, that's why Emojis exist—to help you express yourself!

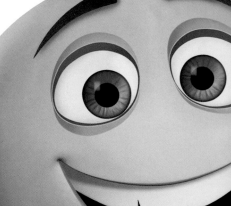